Rustic Style

RUSTIC

Photographs and text by

Ralph Kylloe

April 2007

STYLE

Harry N. Abrams, Inc.,

Publishers

The most beautiful and deepest experience a man can have is the sense of the mysterious.

Albert Einstein, 1932

Editor: Robert Morton
Assistant Editor: Nola Butler
Designer: Robert McKee

Library of Congress Cataloging-in-Publication Data
Kylloe, Ralph R.
    Rustic style / photographs and text by Ralph Kylloe.
      p.   cm.
    Includes index.
    ISBN 0–8109–4432–4
    1. Decoration and ornament, Rustic—United States.
    2. House furnishings—United States. 3. Interior decoration accessories—
    United States. I. Title.
    NK1403.K96   1998
    745' .0973—dc21   98–12075

Printed and bound in Hong Kong

Harry N. Abrams, Inc.
100 Fifth Avenue
New York, N.Y. 10011
www.abramsbooks.com

CONTENTS

ANTECEDENTS

Rustic style did not originate in North America. Nor is it a product of the twentieth century. It could be said that rustic style goes back to our earliest ancestors. In the forests, plains, and savannahs of prehistory early humans lived by their wits and used handmade implements; they kept souvenirs of their hunts and their adventures; they mounted the horns of the great beasts they slew on the walls of their huts. Eventually, to avoid lying on the damp earth or sitting on uncomfortable rock, they made beds and chairs from saplings and the limbs of mature trees. When tools evolved sufficiently to cut wood more precisely, they fashioned tables and storage furniture from planks sawed from lengths of tree trunks.

In time, the furnishings of homes became much more sophisticated. Cities grew up and from Ancient Egypt to modern times, a wide range of styles in furnishing and home decor developed. To some extent, humankind lost its connection with the earth. But the out-of-doors and natural objects held their interest for us. Pets and gardens of various kinds remind us of our connection to the earth. We often vacation in glorious mountain environments and relax by clear waters. Nature calls deeply to our spirits.

And some among us keep hints of nature close by in the form of home furnishings and decoration, whether we live in densely populated modern cities or in a rural setting. More than twenty-five-thousand log cabins are built in North America every year. The Japanese import more than ten thousand log homes each year. Rustic lodges, camps, and cabins have sprung up or have been restored from an earlier life all across America and Europe. Magazines such as *Country Living*, *Architectural Digest*, and many other publications feature rustic settings of the grandest nature on their monthly pages. Rustic style is a way of living, and it remains a part of many of us.

The earliest documentation of rustic furnishings comes from thirteenth-century wood block prints from China. Shown in various prints are several different kinds of tables and chairs fashioned from the roots of trees and with bases of tree stumps. Of course, for centuries, people on all the continents lived with what we would now call rustic style furnishings. The Scandinavian Vikings in their Mead Halls, Africans in their mud-brick huts, Eastern Europeans in their Bohemian hunting lodges, and countless other groups over time used natural materials

At a lean-to in the Adirondacks from early in the twentieth century not much furniture was necessary.

both because they were available and later as a nostalgic reminder of earlier ways of living. In more modern times, wealthy New Yorkers built great camps in the Adirondack Mountains and Americans from both coasts flocked to sample the cowboy lifestyle in dude ranches tucked away in the untouched valleys of the Rocky Mountains.

STYLES

North Woods or Adirondack

When most people think of Rustic Americana they immediately think of the decorative style that characterizes the camps, inns, lodges, and hotels of the six-million-acre Adirondack Park some four hours north of New York City. So pervasive is this stereotype that just about any piece of furniture that has bark on it may be deemed "Adirondack, " albeit incorrectly. Although the Adirondack Park does house some of the most extraordinary rustic architecture, residents of other northern states produced wonderful log structures and rustic furnishings as well. Maine, New Hampshire, Vermont, Michigan, Wisconsin, and Minnesota all have a history of such buildings and a host of furniture makers who provided comfortable and functional environments for their inhabitants.

A prime example of such a maker from Michigan is Raymond W. Overholzer, who created some of the finest examples of rustic furniture in the North Woods. His entire collection is presently housed in the Shrine of the Pines Museum in Baldwin, Michigan, now a National Historic site. Another example of Michigan artistry can be found in the works of Stanislaw Smolak, a Polish immigrant who built the Legs Inn on the shores of Lake Michigan in the town of Cross Village. There, over a period of several decades, he completed several hundred rustic items including all the furnishings for the inn, which he owned, as well as numerous totem poles, wooden sculptures, and other whimsical items.

The northern woodlands are replete with birch, cedar, maple, and other trees, whose bark, roots, trunks, and limbs have provided the raw materials for furnishings since time immemorial. The first makers were trappers, hunters, loggers, and others who came to these woods to make a living. For their own housing they crudely fashioned what they needed from what was at hand. Gradually, as the north woods attracted city dwellers who came to "rusticate" and renew themselves, their caretakers and guides, some of whom had earlier been woodsmen, were asked to build some furniture throughout the long winter months. Some of these workers became highly skilled at this new craft, and they were able to continue building things out of materials that were just outside their back doors. It was, for the most part, simple work. At the same time, however, there were few tools available and often builders had to resort to making their own nails. But the Adirondack guides and furniture makers got the job done and created a fashion that today is considered extremely stylish, fashionable, and collectible.

Beginning in the 1840s, New Yorkers flocked to the Adirondacks for rest, relaxation, and adventure. In 1869 Rev. William H. H. Murray published his now famous book *Adventures in the Wilderness* and the rush was on. Despite difficult travel conditions, the absence of many rooms at lodges, few guides to show the way, and the presence of the annoying black fly, enthusiasm for the region remained high. In the 1880s America's wealthy elite decided that they, too, wanted to partake of the Adirondack experience. Soon Alfred Vanderbilt, John D. Rockefeller, J. P. Morgan, and others built gigantic log and rustic structures with names like Uncas, Sagamore, Kamp Kill Kare, and Top Ridge. Some of the homes built by these individuals were not just small retreats. Rather, architects such as William West Durant and William L. Coulter built huge complexes, Great Camps as they came to be known, capable of housing the families of the tycoons as well as another hundred or so guests, caretakers, guides, cooks, and other support staff.

Much of the charm of Adirondack style lies in its architecture. Whether it be a simple one-room cabin or a great camp, the architecture of the Adirondacks is distinctive. Numerous earlier styles had their influence. Many of the camps reflect Swiss and Scandinavian buildings. And although the interiors may show the more sophisticated influence of the Arts and Crafts or Prairie School movements, it was nature itself that called the tune. Exterior walls, porch railings, staircases, towers, and roof lines incorporated tree trunks, limbs, branches, bark, and roots. With their twists and gnarls the organic components of the Adirondack environment made themselves felt everywhere. North Woods style connects with nature.

Most of these structures were not the principal residences for their owners. Like many second homes, therefore, even for the very rich, they often became repositories for unwanted furniture from other residences. I have been in dozens of these early homes, and it is no longer surprising to me to find them filled with furnishings in a wide variety of styles, including tables, chairs, and other pieces in wicker and Mission (otherwise known as Arts and Crafts) style, Tiffany and Handel lamps, oriental rugs, and all manner of other decorative objects. Needless to say, since these camps were outposts for hunting and fishing enthusiasts, the walls and floors were often decorated with trophies of the sports, paintings and other artwork, and equipment of all sorts related to outdoor pursuits. Even in all its variety, however, a true Adirondack or North Woods style quickly evolved and made its presence known throughout the land.

On the walls of the Great Camps were taxidermy specimens and paintings of animals indigenous to the region. From the ceilings hung chandeliers made from antlers of elk, moose, and deer. Weapons of the hunt rested on wall racks or in glass-fronted cases. Fishing creels and pack baskets were seen on wall hooks or chair posts. Old skis and snowshoes in pairs were crossed and placed over monstrous fireplaces or on the walls of soaring Great Rooms. Canoe paddles were often hung in full display as decorative embellishments and occasionally a canoe was hung upside down from the ceiling.

On the floors were hemp or wool rugs, often made by Navajo Indians. For warmth and color, sofas and chairs were often draped with bright red and black wool blankets woven for the rugged northern life by such companies as Early's, Hudson Bay, Pendleton, and others. Hunting jackets, rain slickers, and a variety of hats made their own contribution to the decor on wall rack racks and coat trees.

The most interesting element of the decor, however, was the furniture. The exteriors of bureaus and other storage pieces were often faced with bark from birch trees. Tables, chairs, benches, and beds were made from cedar or yellow birch trees and many tables, chairs, picture frames and other pieces of furniture were covered in intricate detail with tiny branches in classical mosaic style. And not all the furniture in Adirondack homes was locally made. Very early on, a group of makers in Indiana were exporting a variety of pieces fashioned from the saplings of the ubiquitous hickory trees of the area. Soon, just about every home in the Adirondacks had its share of Indiana hickory.

The dining room of the Old Faithful Inn at Yellowstone National Park
still seats guests on the original hickory furniture puchased in the early 1900s.

Indiana Hickory

No type of furniture is more pervasive within the realm of rustic style than the efforts of the Indiana hickory furniture makers. Beginning in the late 1880s folk artists and craftsmen from Indiana began making simple chairs, rockers, and tables from hickory saplings that were incredibly abundant in the central and southern regions of Indiana.

And no other company had more influence on North American rustic style than the Old Hickory Chair Company of Martinsville, Indiana. Early records indicate that the business was first started by Billy Richardson of nearby Morgantown. There he built simple rustic chairs and tables from hickory saplings. On weekends he loaded his furniture onto a horse-drawn wagon and sold his creations on the town square of Martinsville. In time he was bought out by M. B. Crist and George Richardson. (It is not known if the two Richardsons were related.) Shortly after, the two gentlemen opened a large shop in a deconsecrated church in Martinsville. Within a few years the company was again sold, this time to William F. Churchman and Edmond L. Brown. The business changed hands several times again in its early years until it was purchased by the Patton family of Martinsville, who retained ownership of the firm until the late 1960s.

The rise and growth of Indiana hickory furniture mirrored trends in American life. At the turn of the twentieth century Americans were developing a new ethic. The industrial revolution had created a middle class, and these new families, with leisure time and some disposable income on their hands, took to the wilderness areas of the continent for recreation, inspiration, and comfort. This new public, tired of the overbearing heaviness and formality of the Victorian style and needing a respite from technology, immediately recognized in hickory furniture a ruggedness and beauty that harked back to the pioneering days of the nation. But it was not only the public that recognized the inherent beauty in hickory furniture. Major designers began using hickory furniture in their efforts. Gustav Stickley, the preeminent designer of the time, often used hickory furniture in bungalows. Another designer, Charles Limbert, also known for his Arts and Crafts designs, sold not only his own furniture but Old Hickory as well.

The Old Hickory Chair Company responded to this new interest with canny awareness, and within a few years their products were being sold at all the major department and furniture stores throughout the country. On a weekly basis trainloads of Old Hickory furniture were sent to the Adirondacks to fill the ever-expanding households of the area. In the Rocky and Appalachian Mountains not only private home owners, but proprietors of lodges and hotels were incredibly pleased at the strength and presence of hickory furniture. In the early part of the century the growing National Park System saw in hickory furniture a ruggedness and quality that would in several ways justify uses in many of the new lodges that were being built in such wilderness places as Glacier, Yellowstone, Grand Canyon, and numerous other national parks.

By 1921, the company had grown to provide furnishings for the entire household, including bedding, lighting, a range of dining and living room furnishings, and accessories to match. Realizing that the company was now more than a chair factory, the owners changed its name to the Old Hickory Furniture Company.

In the 1930s the company took a bold leap into the realm of design. They introduced an expensive line of designer pieces of upholstered furniture. The public responded favorably at first and the company further expanded their offerings. During the 1940s prominent modern designers such as Russel Wright were brought into the company to streamline the designs. And streamline they did, but the new products failed to capture the imagination of the public. Old Hickory was known for its ruggedness and strength. Many of the new designs seemed to lack those qualities and were soon dropped.

The company continued, however, to offer their traditional line of very high quality rustic furnishings and the business prospered into the 1960s. Old Hickory then changed hands several times and it was eventually bought out by the Ramada Inn Corporation. At that time the efforts of the company were changed to the manufacturing of hotel furniture, but this new effort proved to be a mistake. In 1972 the company closed its doors.

At its peak, however, the Old Hickory Furniture Company manufactured more than two thousand pieces of hickory furniture each week. This went on for more than sixty-five years. Not surprisingly, there are large amounts of Old Hickory furniture still around, and quite often it is possible to see original pieces in their original settings. As the photograph on page 10 shows, the Old Faithful Inn at Yellowstone Park has more than a thousand chairs still in use. Many other lodges and cabins in the National Park system still have many of the early pieces. Private collectors (the author included) have gathered hickory furniture for many years, and numerous individuals still have hickory furniture on their porches and in their homes.

Research into the age of Old Hickory furniture is an interesting pursuit, and with a bit of study one can guess fairly accurately the age of hickory furniture. All production pieces from the Old Hickory Company were marked with either a burned-in brand, a paper label, or a brass tag. The places to look for such marks are inside the back legs of chairs, or underneath tabletops for any forms of the signature. If the brand reads Old Hickory Chair Co., it was made in 1921 or before. Sometime in the late 1920s or early 1930s the company started applying a small brass tag to many of their products. The tag reads "Genuine Old Hickory, Bruce Preserved, Martinsville, Indiana." In the center of the tag is a number. That number is the year the piece was made. At some point in the 1930s, the company began applying round, metal-edged paper labels to their furnishings, and these appear on many of their offerings until the 1960s.

Other indicators are also available. The 1931 Old Hickory catalogue indicates that this was the first year that the company used wooden "slates" as well as their traditional woven material as seats and backs for their seating products. The 1937 catalogue for the first time

No. 32 "Andrew Jackson" Chair		Price $ 4.00
Height 36 inches, seat 17 inches wide, 15 inches deep		
No. 33 "Andrew Jackson" Rocker		Price $ 4.75
Height 36 inches, seat 17 inches wide, 15 inches deep		
No. 106 Settee		Price $11.00
Height 36 inches, seat 42 inches long, 16 inches deep		
No. 107 Rocker Settee		Price $12.00
Same as No. 106 Settee, with rockers		
No. 199 Table		Price $ 9.00
Height 28 inches, Oak top, 30 inches in diameter, shelf 18 inches Finished Golden Oak		

A page from Old Hickory Chair Company's 1914 Porch and Garden Furniture catalogue

shows an open weave pattern in rattan used on seating products. As the war approached, rattan was the only material used for seating. And the only place it was grown naturally was tropical Asia. Needless to say, the United States stopped importing rattan during the war. Consequently chairs with either all slates, upholstered, or woven with a canvas product are often from that era.

In the 1980s the Old Hickory company was reopened, and today the company is located in Shelbyville, Indiana, just a few miles south of Indianapolis. Each piece of furniture is still handmade. Not only does the company continue to offer the traditional designs and styles from the turn of the century, but they also provide well made, innovative custom designer furnishings. Despite some recent growing pains, brought on in part by success, the increased awareness of the beauty of rustic styling seems to assure the company a busy future.

Although Old Hickory was the largest Indiana company of its kind, numerous other firms have played a significant role in the history of hickory style and design. At least nine other hickory furniture firms have existed during the past hundred years. The city of LaPorte, Indiana, was the home of the Rustic Hickory Furniture Company, which opened in 1902. They offered more than a hundred pieces of very stylish, quite expensive furniture. Like Old Hickory, they sold throughout the country making products which were well regarded by patrons, and are still highly prized by collectors today. Unfortunately, the company closed its doors at the height of the Depression in 1933.

The town of Martinsville, Indiana, was also the home of the Indiana Willow Products Company. Started in 1937 by Emerson Laughner and Clyde Hatley, both former employees of Old Hickory, the company initially manufactured rustic furniture from willow, but later began using hickory because of its strength and durability. The company was responsible for many stylistic and structural innovations in the field.

Other towns in Indiana, including Jasper, Bedford, Columbus, and Colfax were also the sites of hickory furniture manufacturers. Three of these firms went out of business during the hard times of the 1930s, but other hickory companies started up at the height of the Depression. It must have been that skilled workers who were let go decided to chance it on their own. After all, it takes few tools to build hickory furniture, and the material was readily available. Several of these firms, including the Indiana Willow Products Company, survived successfully until the 1960s.

Another company, the Bedford Hickory Furniture Company, was quite visible during the middle part of the century. The company was owned by Luther A. Simons, who had a long history in the hickory furniture business. He was part owner both of the J & S Hickory Furniture Company and the Columbus Hickory Furniture Company. At the Bedford company, Simons got the contract for providing hickory furniture in the chain of roadside stopping places called Wig Wam Motels throughout the country.

Simons' products tend to be heavier in scale than furniture from the other hickory firms. The head and footboards of the beds, as well as the seats and backs of his chairs, are usually woven with a paper weave invented by Simons and made from the by-products of spruce trees. Simonite was used for many years and is still on the market today. The Old Hickory Company still uses Simonite and has found it to be rugged and durable.

Simons also used linoleum on the tops of many of his tables, desks, and bureaus. At the time it was considered very stylish, and was thought to be resistant to liquid spills and the cigarette burns that so often occurred in motels and other places of high use. Luther Simons died in 1951 and the company he founded closed its doors a few years after his death. His furniture, especially his beds and rocking chairs, is considered very desirable to collect.

Among the other makers of hickory furniture in Indiana was the State Prison in Putnamville. Beginning in 1929, the prison turned out high quality rustic furniture. Their gliders, side chairs, settees, recliners, and other furniture are considered to be very well made and exceptionally functional. The prison stopped making rustic hickory furniture in the mid-1960s. A decade later they once again offered hickory furniture, but their recent efforts lack the artistic qualities that were pervasive in their earlier works.

By the last quarter of the twentieth century, except for Old Hickory, all of the Indiana makers of hickory and rustic were gone. The demise of the various firms was brought about by declining interest and the fact that aluminum porch chairs were selling for $5 each and hickory chairs were at that time around $80 each.

Antique hickory furniture finds passionate devotion among collectors. Rugged and solid, many of the early pieces are still available. Often pieces show up at auctions, flea markets, and yard sales. Quite often good quality pieces also show up at country and folk art antique shows. The prices of good antique hickory furniture have escalated dramatically in the past few years. It is expected that the prices will continue to rise as the public becomes further aware of the naturalness, durability, and aesthetics of hickory, making for objects that were once described by eighty-year-old Harold Snyder, a former Old Hickory employee, as "the best gall-darn furniture I ever did see!"

This postcard photograph from 1943 shows the dining room of Battle Mountain Ranch in Jackson Hole, Wyoming with its lodgepole pine furniture, Navajo rugs, and typical mountain resort decorations.

Western or Cowboy

By the middle of the nineteenth century, when America was still quite young, settlers moved into traditional Indian territories in the American West, and a new culture quickly evolved. In the wide-open spaces of the West, with abundant grasslands and broad plains watered by

Opposite, above, and on the following pages: This unique home in the Rocky Mountains at Jackson Hole, Wyoming, was designed by Jim Nagel of Chicago and built by contractor Mike Beauchemin. The furnishings were gathered over a five-year period by the owners, Gail and Don Cook, with the help of Terry

and Sandy Winchell, proprietors of Fighting Bear Antiques, a local gallery.
Above, at left: Among the furnishings are many pieces by Thomas Molesworth, a cabinetmaker of Cody, Wyoming, whose Shoshone Furniture Company flourished in the 1930s.
Above, center: Navajo rugs in the living room

add color, as they do everywhere in the house.
Above, and at right: The huge Great Room, with its grand staircase, is lit by a branding iron chandelier, designed and made by Terry Winchell. Under construction for five years, the house was completed early in 1998.

clear rivers, it was natural that cattle raising would prevail. The United States Army had seen to the demise of the buffalo, so the stage was set for cattle culture. Gradually, a romance grew up around the cowboy. Particularly for Easterners, the allure of the West held great attraction. Newspapers and books glorified Western adventures, and tender-footed travelers with increasing affluence and leisure time rode the rails westward to see the sunsets, ride the plains, watch the herding of the cows, and fish and hunt for the remaining beasts that populated the prairies and mountains.

In the early part of the twentieth century dude ranches exploded onto the scene. In Jackson, Wyoming more than thirty ranches offered amateurs the opportunity to experience the rugged life. Jackson was the stop-off station for several railroad lines and visitors from the East took the train to explore their fantasies of the cowboy style. Jackson was not only blessed with extraordinary wildlife and fishing opportunities but also with a view of the Grand Teton Mountains that still thrills and inspires viewers.

Left:
Behind the curving staircase, with its burled handrails, a back wall opens to reveal a secret staircase leading to rooms below. On a Molesworth table a Black Forest bear keeps guard.

Opposite page:
Top left:
A Molesworth bedroom set rests beneath a 1920s chandelier made from caribou antlers.

Top right:
The remarkable, ornate banister of burled lodgepole pine makes its own decorative statement.

Bottom left:
The tall Black Forest clock was made in Switzerland in the 1870s. As in all Black Forest pieces, the clock's case was made of linden wood.

Bottom right:
A Western painting and original Molesworth furniture fill a corner of the living room.

Upper left:
This sideboard by Molesworth, decorated with Indian motifs and made of local pine, is one of the maker's finest pieces.

Upper right:
An intimate sitting room with an antique European door glows with a Navajo-style rug and authentic Navajo wall hangings.

Above:
One of the largest dining room tables made by Molesworth, this example, with a leather top, seats twelve in matching chairs.

Along with those who made a business of hosting the visitors, many people with crafting skills saw an opportunity. Out of the seasonal westward migration—summer for hunting and fishing, winter for skiing—numerous folk artists, beginning at the turn of the century, created rich environments, based on motifs and designs from Indian and cowboy material culture, where visitors could return to the days of yesteryear.

Log cabins, of course, were the order of the day. And the cabins were furnished with all sorts of Western and Indian memorabilia including baskets, blankets of reds, grays, blacks, and browns, spears, bows and arrows, intricate beadwork, and numerous other distinctively Western rustic decorative accessories.

The Western-style kitchen of
the Cook home features a
heavy counter decorated with
dramatic lodgepole pine
burls.

Initially, several of the early woodworkers created furniture made from the straight poles of the indigenous lodgepole pine trees. The early builders of the period were John Wurtz, Chet Woodward, and Otto and Albert Nelson, who created furniture in the classic rustic style for many of the Jackson ranches. George Rathe, working further north in Montana, created wonderful rustic furniture for the alliteratively named Keens Kozy Kountry Klub and other ranches in the Billings, Montana, area.

In the early 1940s Joseph and Max Kudar opened the Kudar Motel, just off the main square in Jackson, Wyoming. The two brothers created meticulously made furniture, and

The Cowboy Bar in Jackson Hole, Wyoming, built by the Kranenberg Brothers in the 1930s, avowed that it was "The Finest Rustic Bar in the World." Floor shows nightly.

often carved small chips into their furniture to add to the folk art quality of their efforts. The furniture was made specifically for the motel, which is still in operation today offering rooms filled with original Kudar brothers furniture.

As the expertise and skills of local Wyoming furniture makers improved, they branched out and began adorning their furnishings with antlers and with wooden elements distinguished by the presence of burls. The crowning achievement of this new approach, at least in the Jackson area, was the Million Dollar Cowboy Bar. Built in the 1930s by Bob and Jack Kranenberg, the Cowboy Bar remains the defining effort of Western style. Today, the bar has been remodeled, but it continues to delight visitors with its massive burl interior, bar stools with saddle seats, and historical accessories. Added to the pleasure is good food and lively country-and-western music.

Western rustic style in an even more abundant display can be seen north of Jackson in the small town of Dubois, Wyoming. In the old section of town there are unremodeled buildings from the 1930s that are full of romance and ambiance. And at the Rustic Pine Tavern, the most authentic Western bar and restaurant imaginable, the setting has not changed one inch under the pressure of modernity. (The bar still serves delicious buffalo steaks.)

Another splendid rustic experience can be found on the drive west from Cody into the eastern entrance of Yellowstone National Park. Several old ranches still exist there, with their furnishings in all their glory, looking inviting and romantic. I have been fortunate to stay at many of these ranches, and have seen more moose, grizzly bears, and spectacular scenery in the area than I thought possible.

Among the early creators of Western rustic style in this area was Thomas Canada Molesworth of Cody, Wyoming. Molesworth had studied design at the Art Institute of Chicago before he opened the Shoshone Furniture Company in Cody in the 1930s. He was committed to innovation, quality, fantasy, and fun. Inherent in rustic furniture is an element of humor. Molesworth was often known to laugh and chuckle to himself as he worked on pieces of furniture.

Molesworth manufactured wonderfully inventive furniture, complete with burls and decorated with antlers. He was also, however, extremely foresighted as a furniture maker and he looked beyond individual pieces and created complete environments. He made doors, chandeliers, wall sconces, curtains, fireplace irons, rugs, and a variety of other accessories.

Although he was aware of and greatly influenced by modernist design trends, the Arts and Crafts movement, and Prairie School styling, Thomas Molesworth was mostly inspired by his immediate environment and the rich panoply of forms that he found in nature. The Western Style as we know it gives testimony to his innovative genius. Original furniture by Molesworth brings very large prices at auction, and several small Western furniture companies have found significant success offering Molesworth reproductions.

Following the lead of Thomas Molesworth the towns of Cody and Jackson, Wyoming, have become the bastions of Western rustic furniture makers. Each September in Cody all the makers get together and hold the annual Western Design Conference. At that time hundreds of people assemble, exhibit their furniture, and attend numerous professional presentations on style and design. It is an event that should not be missed by those interested in rustic furniture.

Antler and Horn Furnishings

Because of their durability antlers are among the oldest artifacts in human history. Their use as weapons, tools, and objects of sacred significance goes back long before recorded time. Ancestral hunters cut, shaved, carved, and sharpened antlers into spearheads, arrow points, needles, knives, and a host of other tools that have survived for millennia. And among the interesting things about ancient antler artifacts is that toolmaking individuals also incised or cut designs onto the surfaces of antler tools. In short, the decorative use of antlers has a long history.

The earliest recorded use of antlers in furnishings dates from the 1500s. From that time onward, the French, Swiss, Germans, Italians, Scots, Irish, and many other nationalities used antlers as constructive elements in tables, chairs, and many decorative accessories, including, in particular, chandeliers. Around 1800 furniture makers began using antlers for the legs for chairs. In the 1820s the cabinet shop of the Viennese craftsman Josef Danhauser offered a full line of antler furnishings, including sofas and other items. In 1851, visitors to the Crystal Palace Exhibition in London were thrilled at the number of writing desks, candelabras, chairs, sofas, and other furnishings, that were either constructed of or adorned with the antlers from red stag, elk, and other animals. The primary producers of antler furnishings at that time were in Munich and Frankfurt, Germany, with other makers also located in Sweden, England, and Austria.

A lone hunter in the Canadian woods has collected three handsome racks of antlers to decorate his lodgings.

A creative furniture maker of the 1900s incorporated an entire elk's head and four real feet in this sturdy armchair.

The market today offers a wide variety of products including chandeliers and related lighting products, tables, seating furniture, and numerous other items. The majority of antler furnishings today are made with naturally shed antlers. In my own gallery I often have people express concern over the notion that many elk may have had to die to make a chandelier. The concern is natural, but misplaced because all ungulates—elk, moose, deer, and others—shed their antlers once a year in order to grow new and larger ones. The discarded antlers are then collected and many of them are used by craftspeople in the making of furnishings and other decorative objects. In Jackson, Wyoming, for example, the yearly collection of shed antlers on the National Elk Wildlife Refuge is a project of Boy Scout troops from the area, and the auction of thousands of pounds of antlers they collect is a major fundraiser for the Scouts.

In addition to the antlers of indigenous grazing animals of the plains, steer horns have been used by several American furniture makers for chairs, tables, couches, and other pieces since the late 1800s. Many of these makers, quite understandably, were located in Texas, but others plied their trade in Chicago because the stockyards there were the largest in the world and horns were in plentiful supply. In Texas, many of the makers were German immigrant craftsmen, who had come to the American Southwest as farmers and found that it was possible to make furniture as they had done in the old country, taking advantage of the abundance of steer horns they discovered in their new home.

One individual who made a major contribution to the horn efforts here in America was Wenzel Freidrich, who immigrated here from the part of Eastern Europe known as Bohemia. Working in Texas in the 1880s and 1890s, Freidrich offered numerous pieces, including a hall stand that contained thirty-two horns and had a price tag of $250. Many of his pieces were rather extraordinary creations and often upholstered in either cowhide, goat skin, fox, jaguar, or silk. Wenzel Freidrich won numerous awards for his efforts and often sent his pieces to clientele in Europe.

Among the purveyors of horn furniture was the Columbian Catalogue Company. Their products included antler and horn chairs. They not only used horns from Texas steer but also imported extra long horns from Brazil for many of their custom pieces. They also incorporated antlers from both mule deer and white tail deer, and often used the feet of steers as the feet of their chairs. Not content with the extravagant nature of horn and antler as building materials, they richly decorated their chairs with ornate tassels, braided cord, and upholstery in classical Victorian style using both silk tapestry and mohair. Columbian products were not cheap. Chairs were priced between $65 and $85 and their sofas began at $85. In the late 1880s these were substantial prices for furniture.

Horn furniture is at the extreme end of rustic style, but it is considered by many to be extraordinarily stylish and decorative. Good chairs often bring $2,000 to $5,000 at auctions. In the early part of this century numerous national design awards were won by chairs made of horns, and today such chairs and their related furnishings are eminently collectible.

Southern Rustic

Like many rural areas around the United States, the Appalachian Mountains offer a wide variety of folk arts and country crafts, just as they have done for many generations. Just about any weekend in the warm months crafters of all sorts offer their folk art along the secondary roads all across the Southern mountain range. There one can find quilts, whirligigs, goobers, apple pies, as well as twig rockers, settees, and just about anything imaginable.

Beginning at about the turn of the twentieth century, Southern folk artists took advantage of the massive quantities of local rhododendron and mountain laurel stands, as well as the young growth of willow trees, the willow shoots, that were and are dominant throughout the area. In the early years European gypsies who had emigrated to the United States perfected the use of bending willow shoots into functional chairs, settees, and tables. These itinerant craftspeople then loaded their furniture onto horse-drawn wagons and sold their offerings door-to-door to the many hotels, retreats, and new homes that sprang up in the area.

Along with the gypsies, other well known makers of Southern rustic furniture were E. L. Goodykoontz and Joseph Quinn of Sweet Springs, Virginia. They made massive chairs and settees from rhododendron and mountain laurel. Their furniture, which was not necessarily known for its comfort, nevertheless was extremely durable and, thus, served well to furnish porches and other less protected environments.

On the back of this postcard of red cypress furniture from Florida, the maker E. A. Morris of New Smyrna Beach, lists prices of $3 for a settee, $2.50 for a rocker, and $7 for a swing, except $6 when purchased with other items. The buyer is assured that the "wood everlasting" is made to be rained on, but is "chemically treated for preservative purposes."

A curious outside influence entered Southern Rustic Style during World War I, when a group of captured German soldiers (they were actually musicians) were interned in the small town of Hot Springs, North Carolina. The soldiers were a creative lot, and in addition to performing concerts for the surrounding communities over more than three years, they also succeeded in building, with very few tools and out of scrap lumber and driftwood, the tiny town of "Old Heidelberg." This group of structures included quaint log cabins, rustic gazebos, and a variety of related rustic buildings, including a church that could house twenty worshipers at a time. It seems likely that this "town," complete with its benches, tables, chairs, and rockers, influenced folk artists from the area for years to come.

The best known and most prolific rustic furniture builder of the South was Reverend Ben Davis of Mars Hill, North Carolina. Davis was an itinerant Baptist minister, and he spent several months a year away from home preaching to farmers in the small towns dotting the rolling hills of western North Carolina. He was known to ride in a motor vehicle only once. Unfortunately, that vehicle was hit by a Coca-Cola truck, and from that time on the kindly reverend only used his horse as a means of transportation. Travel was apparently a hazardous undertaking for Reverend Davis, and he often stayed in the homes of his parishioners for several months at a time. In exchange for room and board he would often present his custom-made furniture as gifts to the owners for their hospitality, or on the occasion of family weddings or other celebrations.

Davis's furniture is rather extraordinary. Small in scale, his tables, chairs, sideboards, china cabinets, and other pieces are heavily adorned with the chipped and carved roots and branches of the rhododendron and laurel bushes that he collected in a burlap bag as he made his way across the countryside. Davis was a quiet man when he worked, and people learned not to speak to him when he was building his furniture. In the evenings, however, after the day's work was done, he was known to be chatty, and would sit for hours around the evening dinner table and engage all sorts of visitors with conversation.

In the 1920s he was staying with a family in Bakersville, North Carolina. In the middle of the day he fell into unconsciousness, and was thought to have suffered a heart attack. Several people tried to help him although they believed that he was gone. To the surprise of those attending him he slowly regained consciousness. His first words were "I saw the angels." For the next twenty years he made some of the finest rustic furniture in North America.

Davis's pieces have been exhibited in several museums and are in the finest private collections. Because of scarcity and price it is nearly impossible to find Davis furniture today, but his influence on Rustic Style is unmistakable. Several makers today produce re-creations of his furniture.

ACCESSORIES

Personal taste knows no bounds. There is, of course, no correct way to furnish any home, and the same is true of rustic architectural style. I have seen new log cabins decorated with everything from period Queen Anne furniture, to high-style Arts and Crafts furnishings, to up-to-the-minute Italian designer items. It is, and always will be, the spirit of the individual or family that makes the home.

With that said, however, I have to admit that there is a certain pleasure in decorating a room in the rustic style. It all starts, of course, with furniture, and many furniture makers around the country today make rustic furniture that is surprisingly comfortable as well as being good looking. Lester Santos, Old Hickory, Mike Patrick at New West, and others make chairs and sofas upholstered in leather and other fabrics and these upholstered pieces are an absolute delight on which to rest.

But the fun part of rustic decor can often be in adding decorative accessories to the basic elements of the building itself and the major furnishings. Functional objects such as chandeliers, lamps, clothes racks, bookcases, and storage pieces head the list of things that truly round out a home decorated in rustic style. The further addition of nonfunctional, purely decorative

In the early twentieth century photographers often used rustic accessories in their studios.

objects can, however, really bring a house into another dimension of style. And these objects run a wide gamut of types, from snowshoes and antique skis, to canoe paddles and woven baskets of many types.

One item that can be found all across the northern states is antique snowshoes. Earlier in the twentieth century companies such as Tubbs, L. L. Bean, and Snowcraft manufactured snowshoes of all shapes and sizes. The most desirable, however, are the ones made by local Indian tribes in both Canada and the United States. The Micmacs, Penobscot, Malecites, Cree, Tetes de Boule, and other tribes excelled at producing snowshoes of very high quality. In general, the tightness of weave of the leather strips that formed the surface of the shoes as well as the form of the snowshoe is what distinguishes exceptional examples. Snowshoes that are longer than they are wide are referred to as pickerels, or Michigans. Bear paw or beaver tail snowshoes are more round than they are long.

Like snowshows, old wooden skis are often found in rustic houses across the northern United States. Just about every old camp, lodge, cabin, and resort shows pairs of skis hung crossed over fireplaces. The old wooden skis with the leather bindings were often made by companies such as Lund, Northland, and others.

Indian arts and crafts form a large and desirable area of decorative collecting and use. In addition to objects made for tribal use, there are also many other things, still made by hand, that were offered by Indians for sale to travelers or tourists. These include a wide variety of birch bark collectibles, including picture frames, miniature canoes, baskets, hanging racks, and other items. These items, like much of the earlier traditional Indian artwork, were sold on reservations, in trading posts, and in souvenir shops around the country.

Indian basketry, weaving, and beadwork are among the most desirable and beautiful of the many native crafts. The colors and patterns of Indian rugs and tapestries are bold and dramatic, beadwork and quillwork is delicate and remarkably intricate, and baskets combine inventions of form and delicacy of craftsmanship in remarkable ways.

Among larger items made by native craftsmen that sometimes find their way indoors and into rustic houses are canoes. The most prized canoes are early birch bark canoes made by a variety of tribes, including the Ojibwa, Tetes de Boule, Algonquin, Iroquois, Cree, Malecite, Kennebec, Passamaquoddy, and many others.

Many of the early Indian canoe builders had significant expertise in both building canoes and decorating them. Their canoes are adorned with a variety of symbols including stars, moose, owls, trees, tepees, and other organic and geometric patterns. The scarcity and high price of many of these early canoes makes them difficult to acquire, but there are individuals around the country today who are building new birch bark canoes. Of course, the modern canoes lack much of the charm of old canoes.

Because of the scarcity and cost of old birch bark canoes, the most widely seen canoes (at least for decoration) are wood and canvas canoe models that were being built in the early part of the twentieth century. Companies such as Old Town, Peterborough, Waltham, and others made beautiful canoes with ribbed interiors. The most desirable (and most expensive) of these are canoes with extra long decks. Usually made of mahogany, the decks add a sense of high style and drama to the canoe.

Used as decorative objects in a house interior canoes have a limited function. Clearly, it takes a room with a very high ceiling to hang a canoe, and a sixteen-foot-long boat is a very awkward thing simply to place in a corner. Nevertheless, canoes are being hung in offices, living rooms, dining areas, on porches, and in just about any room of many houses. One interesting variant on using a canoe indoors happens when an old canoe has damage at one end.

These boats are then cut to remove the damage, inverted on the cut end and stood up to be made into bookshelves. The shelves are then used in any room in the house and are great for storage or displaying books or collections of small objects. Some outdoor retailers around the country, including, L. L. Bean, Orvis, Eddie Bauer, and others have used cut-off canoes for retail display space as well.

Canoe paddles are now also collectible and very decorative. Hung on walls, their forms add a certain ambiance to nooks and corners. And, as with snowshoes, the most desirable paddles are those made by Indians. With their circular and fitted handles and narrow blades they

Pack baskets like those in the foreground of this 1930s inland Maine fishing scene may have been made by local Indians.

offer a sense of sophisticated style and design. Commercial producers of canoes such as the Old Town Canoe Company, the Peterborough Canoe Company, and others are also sources for old canoe paddles that have become quite collectible.

Among the most desirable old canoe paddles are those made from bird's-eye and tiger maple. These woods are highly figured and offer dramatic accents to any room. Although they are hard to find and quite expensive, I have collected these paddles for the past ten years and have only seen eight great ones during that time. I managed to buy seven of the eight. But good canoe paddles are available at many flea markets around the country. An interesting variant to look for are paddles that have been painted by a former owner. Many children's camps around the country encouraged campers to decorate their canoe paddles as part of the afternoon arts and crafts program. Surprisingly, many of these painted paddles are quite decorative. They also offer a challenge to the collector to find the interesting ones.

Fishing creels and Adirondack pack baskets are now considered very desirable as decorative accessories in a rustic home. Prices for these items have shot up dramatically during the past few years as individuals have sought to upgrade their collections with finer examples. Indian handmade creels of oak, willow, ash, or splint top the list of desirability. Special prizes are the handmade, leather-trimmed, turtle creels by Ilhan Nu of Colorado or the hand-tooled, leather-trimmed creels of George Lawrence of Oregon. Both men produced extraordinary creels until the 1940s. Again, however, commercial sellers of creels such as L. L. Bean, Orvis, and others have offered high quality American creels and Japanese splint creels which are highly collectible today.

Pack baskets have caught on with collectors during the past few years. The most desirable ones have dramatic forms and contours. Also desirable to find are baskets with their original leather straps or the canvas coverings that kept the pack and its contents dry on rainy days. Occasionally one may find a creel or pack that has been painted, usually in reds, browns, and other earth colors. Some purists are averse to collecting "paint," but early painted packs and creels can make striking additions to rooms that seem to need a touch of color. After all, most rustic architecture and furniture is basically monochromatic. I wouldn't, therefore, hesitate to buy or use such a colorful object, but I would look for something that has original paint on it.

Preserved and mounted animal trophies, loosely called taxidermy in the rustic trade, have found interest among many collectors and decorators around the country. In my own gallery we offer a wide assortment of taxidermy, as well as items made from antlers and horns. One has to be careful, of course, because it is illegal to own or sell ivory or skins of many species of animals whose existence is endangered, and none of us want to contribute to the problem by encouraging a market in prohibited hunting or trapping. As for antlers, however, there is no such problem, because animals are not slain for them. All elk, moose, deer, caribou, reindeer, and other animals that carry antlers lose them naturally once a year in order to grow larger ones. Shed antlers are routinely collected on wildlife refuges, game parks, and on farms where ungulates are raised commercially. In my own gallery we use naturally shed antlers in the construction of our furniture. I find that mounted antlers and horns offer some of the most compelling forms in nature.

Another category of decorative objects from the rustic past are old camp signs. They can be fun to collect and exhibit. Reminding us of more innocent times, they speak of happy connections with relaxation, camp fires, old friends, and outdoor adventures wonderful to remember.

The list can go on and on, but whatever one buys to help create an atmosphere of rustic style it should be a rule to make sure that everything purchased is in excellent condition, is aesthetically pleasing, and is comfortable if it is to be functional.

Rustic settings are best created and composed from our own instincts. Decorating in the rustic style is fun. Humor and freedom abound in nature. Each of us longs to feel the passions of nature and each of us can fathom the depth of our own connection with the earth if we spend just a little time contemplating the sweet smells of the earth, the complexity, enormity, and peace of the forest, and the delightful sensation of sunlight on our bodies. Adventure is in our hearts. We cannot deny our own past.

Rustic Style is not an academic pursuit. We need not spend years researching the subtle differences between various cabinetmakers or metalsmiths. Further, most of us with available time do not need to hire decorators to do what we know by instinct. In us all are the secret messages of nature. It is natural for us to live this way. We all hear the call. It is from whence we came.

Living Rooms

A hand-hammered iron wall sconce and a cedar liquor cabinet in the Adirondack home of interior decorator Barbara Collum add to the rustic ambiance provided by a collection of wooden waterfowl decoys.

Opposite:
At the home of the author in Lake George, New York, an extensive collection of Adirondack memorabilia, including pack baskets, fishing creels, camp signs, picture frames, and furniture, form part of the rustic style. The sofa table was made by Peter Winter; the hammered-copper lamp is by Michael Adams.

A clock by Jerry Farrell and
an antler chandelier by
Tom Welsh join furniture
designed by the author in the
Arts and Crafts style at his
Adirondack home.

Spotted Horse Ranch, just
outside Jackson, Wyoming, is
filled with original Western
furniture and accessories
such as taxidermy specimens
and other memorabilia.

Opposite:
This original hall stand by
Barney and Susan Bellinger
of Sampson Bog Studios has
been made with antique oars
for the legs. Trimmed with
moose antlers and antique
fishing pole handles, the
piece is covered with birch
bark and trimmed out with
maple and elm twigs. The
painting in the door panel
is by Barney Bellinger.

Opposite page:
Upper left:
Furniture in what is known as the Whitney Cabin, named for a local mountain, at the Lake Placid Lodge in upper New York State, was designed by the author. The lodge has several small historical lakeside cabins as well as a central Great Camp building for the enjoyment of guests.

Upper right:
The Fisherman's Cabin at Manka's Inverness Lodge in Inverness, California, offers rooms and cabins with antique rustic furniture made by the Old Hickory Furniture Company, as well as a variety of camp accessories.

Bottom:
The boathouse owned by Barbara Collum was built in 1915 by local architect Augustus Shepard. The Great Room is furnished with antique wicker, birch bark, and cedar furniture as well as Adirondack memorabilia.

Here, at right:
The sideboard, used in a home in the Rocky Mountains and made of lodgepole pine, was built by Doug Tedrow of Ketchum, Idaho. A contemporary Arts and Crafts style floor lamp stands beside it.

Above:
The furniture in this
contemporary stone
mansion was built by Lester
Santos of Cody, Wyoming.
Worked in the classical
"cowboy" style, the furniture
blends naturally into this
Rocky Mountain setting.
Navajo rugs are displayed
over the banister.

Opposite, below:
Many early twentieth-
century vacation homes
were furnished with
then-contemporary
furniture made by Gustav
Stickley, the Old Hickory
Company, and numerous
other makers. Various
furniture styles and
Navajo rugs blend well
together in the Adirondack
lakeside home.

Above:
A small rustic retreat in
New Hampshire offers a
fine setting for the owner's
collection of Frederick
Remington bronzes seen
atop the mantel and flanking
the fireplace. The cabin,
built in the 1920s, was refur-
bished in the early 1980s.

Opposite:
A cowboy-style living room
in the shadows of the Grand
Tetons features cowboy boots
as display objects, a not-
uncommon contemporary
Western practice. The rocker
was constructed from local
pine trees and woven with
rawhide. A distinctive architectural feature in this dramatic room is the heavily
burled mantelpiece.

The sofa table made of
lodgepole pine was made
by Doug Tedrow. Many
traditional homes are incorporating rustic furniture
into their settings. A Tiffany
lamp dating from the early
years of the twentieth
century fits in as well.

This lodgepole log chair is
the favorite evening resting
place of rustic furniture
maker Doug Tedrow. Cowboy
hats and other related
accessories add up to classic
Western decor.

Opposite page:
The staircase in the home of the author is red pine; the newel posts are made from apple trees. Antlers are those of reindeer and caribou. The birch bark cupboard beside the staircase was made by Randy Holden of Skowhegan, Maine.

Left:
The original living room of the Pahaska Tepee Lodge, once owned by Buffalo Bill Cody, still stands just outside the east entrance to Yellowstone Park. The lodge was built in 1904. Now open to the public, and with its original furnishings, the lodge, whose name comes from Sioux language meaning "Long Hairs Lodge," offers several cabins, meals, and many outdoor activities.

Below left:
This solid cherry sideboard by Lester Santos features carved scenic door panels, a characteristic of the maker's style. The legs and moldings are juniper. Throughout the years, furniture made by Lester Santos has shown consistent originality.

This settee was built by Michael Hutton of Pittsfield, Illinois, who creates inlays of maple, oak, and pine for the seats and backs of his chairs in a variety of geometric and scenic patterns. The frames of the chairs are usually of elm or cedar.

Right: Barney Bellinger painted this trout scene and made a frame of natural materials. The artist often incorporates such paintings in furniture pieces.

Shrine of the Pines Museum in Baldwin, Michigan, preserves the work of Raymond W. Overholzer, including this rocking chair, which is so well balanced that it will rock fifty-five times on a single push.

This unique pair of arm chairs was designed and built by Overholzer in the 1920s. As can be seen, the chairs were made by hollowing out the trunks of locally cut white pine trees.

Barney Bellinger created this fly tying desk that graces the reception area at the Lake Placid Lodge in Lake Placid, New York. The desk, constructed with yellow birch legs, offers a number of small drawers that suit its use. Typical of work by Bellinger, the piece includes a small painting, here an Adirondack scene.

Offices and Work Areas

Absaroka Mountain Lodge in East Yellowstone Valley, Wyoming, was built in 1910 and contains original furnishings made of lodgepole pine along with a variety of authentic Western accessories. The resort, whose office is shown here, lies just a few miles from the eastern entrance to Yellowstone National Park.

Opposite:
A bedside desk in an apartment in Maine contains an interesting variety of rustic decorations, including painted miniature canoes, painted paddles, and an old toy church of twigs. The hickory furniture was made in Indiana in the 1930s.

48

Clockwise this page:
A bookcase and umbrella stand in the Arts and Crafts style and made from hickory saplings was manufactured by the Old Hickory Chair Company. The furniture, bought in 1909, has stood in the same spot in the study of an Adirondack Great Camp since it was purchased.

A living room rocker and chair by Brent McGregor of Sisters, Oregon, are made of burled lodgepole pine, oak, white birch and elk antlers.

A home office on the shores of a New Hampshire pond is the workspace of an investment banker who takes full advantage of modern business communications as he watches moose wander through his front yard. The Canadian canoe in the rafters was made in the 1930s.

Opposite page:
A study nook shelters a rare comb-back hickory rocker, so called for the high extension on the back that resembles old-fashioned women's hair combs. The antique floor lamp made from elk and moose antlers has a mica shade.

Opposite:
About 1910 the Old Hickory Chair Company offered a line of pieces made of hickory saplings and oak that sold for between $40 and $160, quite expensive for the time. Other objects sold for as little as $5. The desk shown here was priced at $40 in the 1910 catalogue. The extensive use of spindles on the desk suggests an Arts and Crafts influence. Only two examples of this desk are known. This one, found in a house beside a New Hampshire lake, presently serves as a telephone desk in the home of the author. The other is in one of the Great Camps in the Adirondacks.

Above:
This distinctive table and stools was designed and constructed by Phil Clausen of Coquille, Oregon. The table was carved from the base of a thousand-year-old maple tree. The stools, lamp, and mirror frame were also made from ancient maple trees.

Above right:
The original foreman's desk from the Old Hickory Chair Company of Martinsville, Indiana, was used in the factory between 1905 and 1920. It was recently found in a basement in Indiana. The company changed its name to Old Hickory Furniture Company in 1921.

Right:
This desk and chair of willow shoots and birch bark was made in the 1920s.

INSPIRATION

The great rustic furniture makers get their ideas from nature. In general they don't say "I'm going to make a chair," and then go out to find the wood. More often than not, nature itself dictates to the builder exactly what is to be built. In the West, for example, the lodgepole pines, with their straight lines and soaring spirit of strength, spoke to builders. The trees seemed the perfect building material. As builders gained more confidence in themselves they experimented with many of the aberrations that they found in both the pines and junipers. The burls and contortions common to both species attracted the eyes of many builders and demanded that they be incorporated into the Western rustic furniture. The burls and bends on many pieces of wood are, in reality, incredibly feminine. Diana Cole, a well known rustic builder from Cody, Wyoming, once commented to me that it was surprising to her how many men undertook the task of building rustic furniture considering how feminine wood really is. Nature, it seems, speaks to both men and women.

Trees offer some of the most compelling forms in all of nature: they dance as they sway to the rhythms of the winds; they stand as monuments of strength and nobility; they are capable of withstanding fire and other hazards that would kill any other living being. Trees are monuments of persistence and tenacity. Trees have provided homes for thousands upon thousands of generations of human beings.

And so humble rustic furniture makers travel through the forest seeking inspiration. Carl Sagan, astronomer and evolutionary-biologist, commented in his last book, *Billions and Billions*, that "nature is far more inventive, subtle, and elegant than humans are." It only stands to reason, then, that we should often retreat to nature itself for inspiration.

RUSTIC DEFINED

In general rustic furniture is made from organic material that maintains its original contours, shapes, and texture. There is usually no attempt to hide the burls, knots, twists, or gnarls with which nature has stamped trees. Under normal circumstances the bark is left on the wood and little attempt is made to manipulate the materials in any way. When I look at a rustic chair I know what sort of wood it is.

The same is true for other organic materials. Antlers are a classic example. The natural forms of antlers are so sensual, so perfect, that there is no need to try to improve on the delicate forms of nature. The piece is used exactly as it is found. A number of rustic artists are today also using materials like pine cones, platform mushrooms, and bark peeled from a variety of different trees. Roots, limbs, twigs, and branches become functional art.

Windblown pine trees like this one with its curves and twists offer inspiration and materials to rustic furniture makers.

RUSTIC FURNITURE MAKERS

Back in the late 1960s a number of people around the country recognized the inherent beauty in many of the antique rustic pieces that were seen in museums, wilderness resorts, and private residences. As a result of this new interest they began asking local craftspeople to produce a few items for them. In time rustic furniture captured the hearts of a number of talented individuals around the country who brought passion, skill, professionalism, and imagination to the realm of rustic woodworking.

Surprisingly, the best rustic furniture makers in the country are not woodworkers by original training or profession. Barney Bellinger, who owns Sampson Bog Studios, was originally a sign painter. Lester Santos of Cody, Wyoming, was once a guitar maker. Barry Gregson was a

Burls on lodgepole pines are a favorite natural form for Western or Cowboy rustic furniture makers. The burls and a section of limb or trunk are either incorporated as chair or table legs or cut off and applied as decorative adornments on furniture.

stonemason. Phil Clausen worked as both a farmer and real estate broker. Jerry Farrell played honky tonk piano for a traveling circus. Clifton Monteith was in the advertising business in Manhattan. Ron Shanor ran a landscaping business. Jimmy Covert was a farmer and ran a sawmill before he moved to Wyoming to build furniture. Brent McGregor of Oregon was an adventurer living in Alaska who ran a line of sled dogs.

Varied in their origins, they bring a unity of extraordinary talent to the medium of rustic furniture making. Jimmy Covert is permanently represented by one of his pieces in the Buffalo Bill Historical Center in Cody, Wyoming. Barney Bellinger is widely regarded as the most accomplished and innovative builder in the East. Ron Shanor has won awards at the Western Design Conference. Barney Bellinger, Clifton Monteith, Jerry Farrell, and others are frequently seen on the pages of *Architectural Digest, Country Living,* and numerous other magazines.

Being a gallery owner, the author of six books, numerous articles, and having lectured all over the country on the subject of rustic furnishings and lifestyles, I receive calls and letters daily from aspiring rustic furniture makers wanting me to see their creations. Unfortunately, much of what I see lacks the sophisticated design and construction techniques evident in the products of accomplished builders. In my files I have photographs and correspondence from more than a thousand aspiring builders. In general, I offer encouragement and make suggestions, among other things recommending that the newcomers visit more accomplished builders in their area. Once in a while, however, a few new people come along who have great talent.

On one occasion I received a call from a woman in Illinois saying that she thought her boyfriend had great talent as a furniture maker and only needed a few tips on marketing, and so forth. I politely asked to see some photographs of his work, and when they arrived I was quite taken with his efforts. The following week I was in Illinois and I visited Michael Hutton at his home in the rural farm country in the middle of the state.

When I pulled off the dirt road and stepped onto the porch of the Hutton farmhouse I was almost shocked to see the quality of Michael's work. The settees and armchairs were exceptionally comfortable. The pieces were all well constructed and the designs were innovative, original, and fun. I bought every piece he had and ordered several more.

Some areas of the country have little interest in rustic furniture. Michael Hutton was no beginner; he had been constructing these chairs and tables for the past thirteen years, had exhibited them at several local shows and fairs, and had sold only a few pieces in his entire career. Needless to say, he was quite discouraged. But like the true artist he is, he rose to the challenge. Hutton, a veteran of the war in Vietnam, is unique in character and, like other accomplished builders, has been successful at other endeavors. Against all odds and against

A rustic furniture maker of the 1890s brings his products, and his family, to market.

the advice of engineers, he constructed by hand a sixteen-inch telescope. He knew the stars like the back of his hand. He also plays exceptional guitar. He is a man of few words, but when I asked him about his future plans, he repeatedly commented that he wanted more than anything to continue making rustic furniture. He told me that he dreamed at night of different designs for his furniture.

Other new furniture makers have also come out of apparent obscurity. Doug Tedrow of Ketchum, Idaho, is making extraordinary furniture with innovative woven wood in Western style. Peter Winter, who worked with Barney Bellinger for two years, now creates absolutely wonderful furniture in the Adirondack style. Tom Welsh, also from the Adirondack region, began making exceptional antler chandeliers recently to complement his burl furniture. Thom George of Oregon makes wonderful furnishings out of willow shoots. Thom is a captivating storyteller as well as an accomplished furniture maker. He recently told me of a hair-raising experience when he was forced to climb a very small tree to escape the jaws of a mountain lion near his home. The big cat kept him up the tree for almost two hours and only left when it spotted a cow and her calf on in the distance.

It may seem that men get all the credit. Male rustic furniture makers, it should be clearly stated, are not alone in the world. Among the major builders, the wives and "significant others" of these men play an important and often instrumental role in the production of rustic artistry. Linda Covert, the wife of Jimmy Covert, does all the leatherwork and upholstery on the products they make together. Susan Bellinger of Sampson Bog Studios runs the office and works on the production of many pieces. Jessica Farrell does all the paintings for husband Jerry's mosaic furniture. Janice Smith works with Doug Tedrow and is responsible for all the finishes on his work. Kara Mickelson, "right-hand-person" to Brent McGregor, is responsible for all finish work and collects materials for many of the amazing pieces that come out of their shop. Beth Humphries, who specializes in birch bark and mosaic work, has become a well respected rustic furniture maker in her own right. Cloudbird George of Sweet Tree Rustic no longer lives in her husband's shadow. Cloudbird makes wonderful lighting from willow trees and does exceptional leatherwork including shades, pillows, and other interesting items. Diane Cole manufactures her own furniture in innovative Western designs.

A few doubting Thomases have spoken disparagingly about the rustic builders of today, saying that they are only making reproductions. Nothing could be further from the truth. Most of the rustic furniture of today is far superior, at least in terms of construction techniques, to the furniture of the past. Certainly there are people throughout the country manufacturing copies from earlier styles. One could say that the Old Hickory Furniture Company is an example of this, but like many other manufacturers they are simply continuing an original tradition. They have been in business for more than a hundred years, and to suggest that they are just making copies of something that they have manufactured for decades does not do justice to their heritage. More importantly, many of the above mentioned individual artists offer significant innovations. They have their own interpretations of what a bed or a chair should look like. At their best they are creating original art at its finest.

Rustic furniture builders of today are an unusually talented group. Their interests are not restricted to their particular area of expertise. I've discovered that it is possible to discuss a wide variety of topics with these men and women, and I'm always a bit surprised at the depth of knowledge of just about every one of them. I've spent hours and hours talking with the major people about art history and philosophy, psychology, astronomy, astrophysics, politics, classical music, literature, and numerous other areas of interest. Rustic furniture makers are far from country bumpkins. Rather, they are a group of sophisticated, talented people who just happen to be in love with rustic furniture. They could very well take their talents elsewhere and succeed in any number of other areas of interest. I'm glad they stuck with rustic furniture. The world is a better place because of them.

Dining Rooms and Kitchens

Burls from lodgepole pine
trees are often used as bases
for dining room tables.
Because of the shapes of
their backs, chairs such as
these are often referred to as
keyhole chairs. The set was
made by Lester Santos of
Cody, Wyoming.

Opposite:
A fallow deer antler
chandelier lights the dining
room of a traditional home in
Ketchum, Idaho. The chairs
and table are Italian. Many
decorators around the country are incorporating rustic
furnishings into traditional
living environments.

Opposite page:
An antique lodgepole pine sideboard stands in the dining area of the Absaroka Mountain Lodge, a small dude ranch just outside Cody, Wyoming. The chairs are woven with rawhide. The ranch was completed in 1910 and the original furnishings are from the 1930s.

Top left:
In this dining area of a stone home in the Rocky Mountains, the chairs were made by the Old Hickory Furniture Company and are woven with rawhide. The sideboard is late Victorian, and made of walnut and rosewood. The top of the dining table was fashioned from old barn boards found near the property.

Bottom left:
In the dining room of this Western style home in Jackson, Wyoming, the table is made of Douglas fir, chairs are of local pine, and the chandelier was fashioned from an old wagon wheel. The cigar store Indian is the handiwork of local artists.

Handmade in the Appalachian
Mountains, probably in the
1920s, this dining room set,
put together with square-cut
nails, was found at auction in
New Jersey in 1992. Made of
rhododendron and mountain
laurel branches, the set has
mellowed to a rich brown.

This dining room set was
made by Reverend Ben Davis of
Mars Hill, North Carolina,
in the 1920s. The legs are of
yellow birch adorned with small
branches of rhododendron.
These chairs show Davis's
tendency toward small scale.

This sideboard was made by the Old Hickory Furniture Company in celebration of its one-hundredth birthday, when the company reissued ten of their early designs. The Centennial Collection piece is made of solid oak and hickory branches. The front of the doors are woven with a product called Simonite, invented in the 1930s by Luther A. Simons, who was owner of three hickory furniture companies in the 1930s and 1940s.

Overleaf, left:
In this Adirondack dining room, the antique chairs and rare corner cupboard are by the Old Hickory Furniture Company. Old camp signs and other memorabilia add to the decor of the room. The chandelier was made from naturally shed antlers of fallow deer by Tom and Bill Welsh of upstate New York.

Overleaf, right:
This contemporary kitchen–dining room in a spacious Adirondack home designed by Michael Bird of Saranac Lake, New York, shows off the post-and-beam construction using old beams. The dining table has cedar legs and a wide, pine board top. The chairs are by the Old Hickory Furniture Company.

Opposite:

This contemporary food server, shelf, and mirror adorned with birch bark were made by Peter Winter, who often uses pine cones, antlers, and other organic material to embellish his pieces. The tops of Winter's pieces are often made of quarter-sawn oak, bird's-eye, maple or other hardwoods.

A North Carolina home boasts a twelve-piece chestnut dining room set made in the 1930s by Reverend Ben Davis. The set includes a dining table and six chairs, a china cabinet, three small tables, and this sideboard, adorned with chipped, carved mountain laurel and rhododendron roots and twigs.

A 1930s china cabinet by Reverend Ben Davis is characteristically small in scale and highly adorned.

Looking as if it would be at home in the desert Southwest, this Ohio kitchen-dining area is furnished by Brent McGregor. The chairs are of pine and upholstered in rawhide.

Right:
Among the hickory
furniture made in the
1920s by the Rustic Hickory
Furniture Company of La
Porte, Indiana, this
dining table with several
leaves opens to seat ten

people. The top is oak
and the base and chairs
are hickory saplings. The
weaving on the chairs, as
on many like them, is of
rattan. The maker went
out of business in 1934.

Above:
Barry Gregson fashioned
this dining room set with a
maple top. Gregson is widely
known for creating especially
comfortable chairs built
completely by hand with
no nails or glue.

A distinctively original pair of dining room armchairs by Barry Gregson. Barry and his son, Matt, build chairs in a variety of woods, including maple, oak, ash, and apple, with seats often carved from butternut or maple.

This small cedar table and chairs were made by East Coast Indians. Marvin Davis, co-owner of Romancing the Woods, a company that specializes in rustic outdoor structures, uses the set in his contemporary home in Woodstock, New York.

Opposite, upper right: An antique cedar cupboard from the Rangeley Lakes area of Maine houses part of the author's collection of more than five hundred antique picture frames made of birch bark and laced with sweet grass.

Right:
This contemporary cupboard
was handcrafted by Peter
Winter of Northville, New
York. Covered with birch

bark, it is decorated with
split branches of maple.
The hammered copper
lamp was made by Michael
Adams of Aurora, New York.

This dining room set by Raymond W. Overholzer was made in the 1920s of locally cut white pine. The base of the table was fashioned from a seven-hundred-pound white pine tree stump; its top is inlaid with more than sixty pieces of pine. At the time of its completion, Henry Ford offered Overholzer $50,000 for the set, but for unknown reasons the craftsman declined. It is presently on display at the museum called Shrine of the Pines in Baldwin, Michigan.

Legs Inn in Cross Village, Michigan, was created by Polish immigrant Stanley Smolak, who spent several decades building it. The furnishings are made mostly from driftwood that washed up on the shores of Lake Michigan, just a few steps from the back door of the inn. The inn has a host of rustic furniture, as well as hundreds of pieces of whimsical folk art, including totem poles, and wooden sculptures of all kinds.

Far left:
Phil Clausen of Oregon made this dining room set from ancient maple trees. The tree trunks that Clausen works with are often so enormous that they are delivered to his workshop on a flatbed truck with a crane.

Left:
Michigan craftsman Raymond W. Overholzer made this extravagant sideboard in the 1920s.

Rustic accents enliven a contemporary kitchen in Ketchum, Idaho. The hanging lamps are from the Mica Lamp Company in California, a contemporary maker. The birch bark canoe was exhibited at the 1932 Chicago World's Fair.

Lionel Maurier of Meredith,
New Hampshire, crafted the
distinctive white birch bark
cabinets for this kitchen.
The counter stools are
of solid maple.

The white birch bark
cabinets in this kitchen are
also by Lionel Maurier.
The delicate rocker, resem-
bling the bent wood style of
European Thonet furniture,
was made by Amish families,
probably in the 1940s.

These contemporary plates
are produced by United
Crafts of Greenwich,
Connecticut. The matte
green finishes and pine
cone motifs blend well into
rustic or Arts and Crafts
settings. The antique antler
handle cutlery was made in
Germany in the 1920s.

Overleaf left:
The old-fashioned kitchen
of rustic furniture maker
Doug Tedrow of Ketchum,
Idaho, centers on a large
cast iron stove.

Overleaf right:
A working cast iron stove also
warms the kitchen of rustic
artisans Brent McGregor
and Kara Mickelson in
Sisters, Oregon.

Opposite:

A cupboard by Barney and Susan Bellinger incorporates a variety of different elements. Bellinger pieces often contain paintings as well as antlers, fly rods, oars, fishing reels, and other things. They are often made of distressed or abraded wood that contains knots and other flaws that add character to the pieces.

Antlers find many uses in this small cabin in Colorado.

In this kitchen in Jackson, Wyoming, stools topped with saddles serve well at the counter. Chairs made by Thomas Molesworth in the 1930s are more comfortable. The rugs are Navajo.

In the author's home kitchen
three-foot-wide slabs of white
pine were used for the coun-
tertops, the custom cabinets
are faced with pine wainscot-
ing, and the handles on the
cabinets and drawers are
made of deer antlers. The
chandelier, fashioned from
an apple tree limb, features
antique shades of green
cased-glass, in which green
panes are encased over white.

The birch bark covering
these kitchen cabinets is
surprisingly resilient in daily
use. The kitchen serves the
home of a summer camp
director in upstate New York.

Bedrooms and Bathrooms

Earnest Stow was a very active cabinetmaker in the Adirondacks in the early 1900s. This original Stow bureau, built around 1902, still serves the family of its original owner in the Adirondacks. Stow's pieces were often made of discarded wood and covered with white birch bark. Here the trim and inlay work is yellow birch.

Opposite;
In this Wyoming bedroom, the lodgepole pine armoire, created by Rob C. Hink of Bellevue, Idaho is literally footed, as can be seen, with boots. The bed sports Beacon blankets from the 1930s.

Opposite:

In another view of the bedroom shown on page 87, the corner fireplace mantel holds some of the owner's collection of kachina dolls along with an original Edward Curtis photograph.

A high-ceilinged Western bedroom features a barnboard cupboard and bunk beds framed with lodgepole pine trunks.

An armoire by Doug Tedrow hides numerous games, electronic devices, and clothing. Tedrow created the woven pattern on the surface of the armoire with small square and rectangular sections of pine.

A contemporary burl wood vanity by Ron Shanor of Cody, Wyoming, has a distinctive look. The highly-figured lodgepole pine adds character.

Max Kudar made most of the original furniture for his motel in Jackson Hole, Wyoming, in the 1930s, and many pieces are still in use. This Western bureau is constructed of chipped, carved lodgepole pine; the drawer pulls are deer antlers.

This contemporary hickory bureau was designed by the author. The hammered copper lamp, with a shade lined with mica, was made by Michael Adams.

The hickory lounge chair and single bed, both made by the Rustic Hickory Furniture Company around 1910, complement other antique hickory furniture in this New Hampshire log home. The blue and white quilt dates from the early nineteenth century and was found in Ohio.

The bed in this New Hampshire log cabin was built by the Rustic Hickory Furniture Company of La Porte, Indiana, in the 1920s. At its foot is an antique birch cube chair found on the porch of a house in the Adirondack Park. The snowshoes on the wall are Indian-made.

Opposite: These birch bunk beds were crafted by Lionel Maurier for an Adirondack home. Between them is a stump-based table by Eric Glesmann of Remsen, New York, and completing the room's decor is a birch bark mirror frame with Indian motifs.

Above and right:
A unique rustic setting,
this room completely lined in
birch bark and furnished
with original beds and
bureaus by John Champney
of the Adirondacks dates
from the early years of the
twentieth century. The use of
birch bark in such extreme
fashion was occasionally
done for pure fantasy, but
of course the material was
readily available and free. In
the photograph above, the
rocker in the right foreground
was made of yellow birch by
Lee Fountain in the 1930s.

Opposite:
A Rustic Hickory Furniture
Company bureau and the
Hudson Bay blankets on the
wall beside it, of a pattern
long known in New England,
both date from the 1930s.

This contemporary hickory bedroom suite was designed by the author and made by the Old Hickory Furniture Company. The rugs are Navajo.

Opposite:
The juniper limbs used in this bed by Jimmy and Linda Covert of Cody, Wyoming, mark the piece as distinctly Western in origin.

BALSAM
ea SOAP
3 FOR 55¢

BALSAM
25¢ea SOAP
3 FOR 70¢

BALSAM 🌲
PILLOWS
Take Home
THE FRAGRANCE
OF THE ADIRONDAKS

Even bathrooms can be
decorated in the rustic
style. At a home in Jackson,
Wyoming, above, the
cabinets are of fir and the
antique furnishings are
made with fallow deer antlers.
The mirror and shelves at
left, in the home of the
author, are believed to have
been made by Peter Winter,
a craftsman of Northville,
New York.

 # Decorative Elements

Trade and architectural
schools at the turn of the
twentieth century often
required their students to
complete small-scale models
of homes before they were
built. Some of these now-
valuable small collectibles
were also made as school or
Boy Scout projects.

Opposite:
Nicely-graduated canoe
paddles from the collection
of Robert Oestreicher,
proprietor of the gallery
known as Moose America, in
Rangeley, Maine, make an
attractive wall hanging.

Above:

A wall of this large room in the Green Mountains of Vermont was decorated with hundreds of thousands of tiny twigs meticulously arranged into patterns. The room was completed in the 1930s and remains unchanged.

Left:

This ornate, multi-story antique miniature log cabin has a roof made from small sections of cedar shingles.

Opposite:

A dining set by the noted furniture maker, Reverend Ben Davis of North Carolina, completed in the late 1920s, consists of the table and six chairs, a china cabinet, and a sideboard. The antique chandelier was made in Europe in the 1920s. The rustic picture frames are from New York's Adirondacks.

Opposite:
A New Hampshire living room features Old Hickory furniture and related memorabilia, including an original furniture advertisement dating from 1924. The sideboard, chairs, lamp, and toys were manufactured between the 1920s and the 1940s. The rug is Navajo from the 1930s.

The yellow birch stump-based table was made by Lee Fountain in the Adirondacks, probably in the 1930s. The miniature chairs are from the Appalachian region and are of mountain laurel twigs.

The breakfast room in the home of Robert Oestreicher in Maine shows off part of his collection of rare fishing creels. The Canadian table and chairs are of cedar.

This diminutive twig table
displays a small mosaic box
from the Adirondacks.

This yellow birch table was
made in the 1920s by
Earl Rector in the
Big Moose Lake area of the
Adirondacks. The antler lamp
wears a mica shade.

Opposite:
A collectors' corner of classic
North Woods objects holds
creels, pack baskets, canoe
paddles, and other items,
and includes a model of an
Old Town Canoe.

Fishing gear mixes with
books in this corner in the
home of the author near
Lake George, New York.

The sideboard of oak and
hickory was designed in the
Arts and Crafts style by the
author. The lamp is by
Michael Adams. Blankets
hanging in the corner
were made by the Beacon
Company in the 1940s, and a
Navajo rug is on the floor.

In the comfortable lounge
area of the Lake Placid
Lodge the furniture is of
hickory and cedar.

This massive rocking chair
bears the numbers of the
house on whose front porch
in Georgia it was found. The
camp signs are from New
England and Pennsylvania.

Overleaf left:
A contemporary chair of
lilac wood made by Barry
Gregson of Schroon Lake,
New York, awaits a guest in
the Lake Placid Lodge.

Overleaf right:
The frame of this remarkable
chair by Michael Hutton of
Illinois is elm; the mosaic
work on the back combines
maple twigs and elm bark.

A hickory lounge chair and a
cluster of rustic accessories
fit perfectly in a New
Hampshire log cabin.

Opposite:
This interesting table, made
in about 1900, comes from
the Adirondacks. Its top has a
mosaic inlay in a geometric
pattern, and the base is from
a yellow birch tree. The lamp
and picture frames are also
from the Adirondack region.

This contemporary root-
based, yellow birch bark table
was made by Sampson
Bog Studios.

An ornate early 1900s root-based table holds a charming scale model settee, probably from Appalachia. The bronze floor lamp is signed Tiffany.

This table, finished in dark varnish and made in the Finger Lakes region of New York, was put together with hundreds of small roots secured with handwrought square-cut nails. Only three examples like it are known. The burl lamp holds an old mica shade. The birch picture frame on the table dates from the early 1900s.

Opposite: This delicate antique table from the Catskill region of New York was made from the branches of mountain laurel shrubs. The lamp is lined with elm bark and has a mica shade from the 1920s.

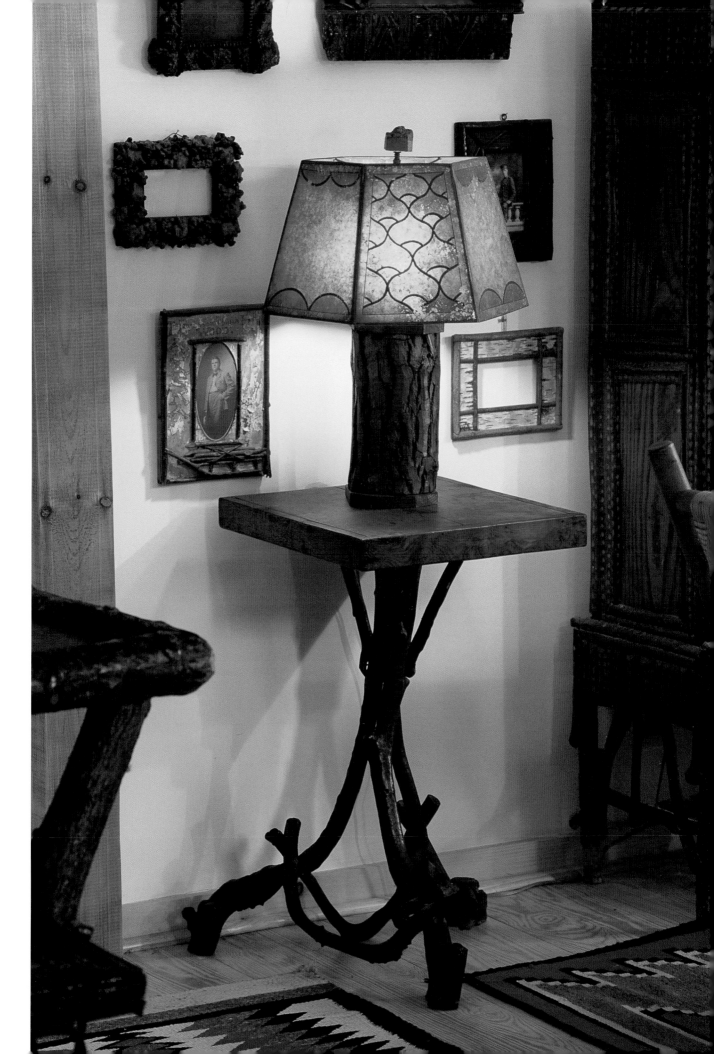

Opposite:

In the trade, the diminutive decorative objects—animal carvings, model tepees and canoes, and assorted other items are known as "smalls."

A classic southern Appalachian rocking chair made either of mountain laurel or rhododendron roots and branches. Despite its appearance the chair is extremely comfortable.

Handwoven fishing creels
were often made by Indians
in New England and upstate
New York and sold to the
tourist trade. The creels
shown here are from the turn
of the century. Creels with
center holes are considered
earlier and more desirable
as collectibles.

This mosaic chair surround-
ed by birch picture frames
was made in the Adirondacks
by Raymond T. Finnan of
Troy, New York, around 1900.

Opposite:
Among these Indian snowshoes
from New England, quality
is judged by the trueness of
form in their frames and the
tightness of the weave of the
leather thongs.

The hand of Reverend Ben Davis marks these twig chairs and lamp. The root table, with a single board chestnut top, is from the Appalachian region. Empty antique mosaic picture frames are hung as art objects.

Compared with the delicacy of much rustic furniture, this contemporary arm chair by Thomas Welsh of the Adirondacks—crafted from cherry burls with back posts of maple—stands out boldly.

Opposite:
Colorful painted antique pack baskets add drama and color to room settings. Beginning around 1900, pack baskets were used extensively in the Adirondacks for carrying personal camping and other equipment, including ice-fishing tools. Occasionally, the baskets were painted or covered with colored cloth to protect them from the elements.

Antler and Horn Furnishings

The wall-mounted letter
holder on the opposite page,
carved in the manner of a
saddlebag and adorned with
carved antlers, was made
in Switzerland in about 1900.
Above is a detail of the
central carving in bone.

Opposite page:
A contemporary armoire adorned with antlers was made by Crystal Farms of Redstone, Colorado, which specializes in antler furniture and decorative objects.

Left:
The antler-decked bedroom ensemble fashioned by Crystal Farms features a headboard, pillows, and lampshade covered in suede.

Below left:
A contemporary antler desk by Crystal Farms has a base primarily of elk and fallow deer antlers, and a top inlaid with leather.

This staircase in a private
home near Jackson Hole,
Wyoming, is adorned with
naturally shed elk antlers.

A large elk antler chandelier
and dramatic wall sconce
light a living room in
Jackson, Wyoming.

A modern office chair was
made in part of elk and
fallow deer antlers.

An elk horn side chair was
made by Chet Woodward in
the 1930s for the Crescent H
Ranch in Jackson, Wyoming.
Cushions for these sorts of
chairs were often covered
with buffalo hide.

Spruced up with new suede cushions, an elk antler chair from the 1930s stands somewhat incongruously beside an African lion skin rug in Ketchum, Idaho. Hunting trophies from different parts of the world often create such discontinuities in rustic style.

Opposite:
Adorned with antlers, the headboard of this bed is covered with suede.

Opposite:

Perhaps the finest piece of antique steer horn furniture in private ownership, this chair makes a favorite resting place in a Rocky Mountain household. The size of the chair, the number of horns, and the condition of the piece distinguish it. Many examples of such furniture made in Texas are now in museum collections.

Above:

As is true with much early rustic furniture, the maker of this elegant steer horn chair from the turn of the century is unknown.

At the Crescent H Ranch,
a retreat for fishermen and
hunters in Jackson, Wyoming,
whose brand can be seen on
the fire screen, the antique
chairs above, and the settees
on the opposite page, are
from the Old Hickory
Furniture Company; they
were recovered several years
ago with steer hides.

John Wurtz made the two elk antler settees and the chair shown here in the late 1920s and 1930s. All are woven with rawhide. The settee at upper right was made for the Spotted Horse Ranch in Jackson, Wyoming.

The window ledge of a Rocky Mountain home boasts a collection of antique Black Forest bears.

Opposite:
A carved wood and antler chandelier by Crystal Farms lights this cozy, high-ceilinged sitting room.

This hall "tree" with three bears comes from a category of rustic furniture known as Black Forest, although none of it was made in Germany. All so-called Black Forest objects were made in Bern, Switzerland, beginning in the 1880s by the family of F. Peter Trauffer. The Trauffers carved all sorts of humorous bear furniture specifically for the tourist trade until the 1950s. Almost all bear furniture is made from linden wood. Bear furniture is being reproduced today and is often found at flea markets and novelty furniture stores. This authentic hall tree is owned by collector/dealers Terry and Sandy Winchell of Jackson, Wyoming.

A graceful elk antler floor
lamp by Crystal Farms seems
almost casually thrown
together.

Opposite:
In the 1930s, Albert Nelson
was a local guide in Jackson,
Wyoming. He lived in a log
cabin, owned a sawmill, and
did taxidermy work. He also
made furniture, including
this pair of floor lamps, with
their delicately carved leaves
of moose antlers, and the
armchair created from elk
antlers and covered with a
bearskin rug.

More examples of furniture
made by Crystal Farms: the
contemporary dining room
chairs and table are made in
part of elk antlers; the antlers
used in the chandelier are of
mule deer, a Western species.

 # The Many Faces of Wood

Beginning in the 1930s, inmates at the state prison in Putnamville, Indiana, were employed in a behind-the-walls factory making furniture of hickory, a readily available local wood. The furniture was well made, rustically stylish, and comfortable. Today it is highly collectible. This porch in New Hampshire shows off a four-piece prison set, including a settee, a pair of arm chairs, and an ottoman: the coffee table is by Old Hickory, another Indiana maker.

Opposite:
One of the Great Camps of the Adirondacks, Top Ridge was built for cereal heiress Marjorie Merriweather Post in the 1920s. The camp is known for its extraordinary rustic design and decor. Still privately owned, the camp is undergoing extensive restoration.

Opposite page:
A porch at Manka's Inverness Lodge in Inverness, California, offers a pair of hickory steamer chairs made in the 1930s by the Old Hickory Furniture Company. The owner of the lodge decided that she did not want to remove any of the mature trees on this side of the building, so she had the porch built around one of them.

Upper left:
On its fortieth anniversary, in 1931, the Old Hickory Company introduced a line of streamlined furniture heavily adorned with spindles. Much of it was also covered with woven rattan. This suite occupies the front porch of a home in New Hampshire.

Middle left:
A long way from home, this handsome pair of antique hickory recliners made in the 1930s at the prison in Putnamville, Indiana, sits on a porch of Manka's Inverness Lodge.

Lower left:
New Hampshire craftsman Lionel Maurier takes advantage of the pruned branches left by caretakers at apple orchards. He collects and uses the apple limbs to build chairs, settees, and tables, employing oak or other hardwood for the seats.

Top:
Just outside Jackson,
Wyoming, this rustic retreat
offers a grand view of
the Grand Tetons.

Above:
Locally cut lodgepole pine
was used for a burled railing
and a rocking chair at this
Rocky Mountain home.

A veranda in the Rocky
Mountains offers painted
pine chairs to sit on and
traditional Southwestern
textiles to please the eye.

Opposite:
A well-known landmark in Yellowstone Park is Hamilton's Store, whose unique front porch features the liberal use of lodgepole pine with dramatic burls.

Below:
Just outside Jackson, Wyoming, artist Greta Gretzinger, who always wanted to live in a log cabin, painted the home of her dreams.

Overleaf, left and right: Staircases at the Old Faithful Inn feature natural organic twists and curves. The inn still maintains all its original furnishings, including more than a thousand chairs by the Old Hickory Company, as well as pieces by Arts and Crafts designers Gustav Stickley and Charles Limbert.

Among many contemporary
sources for outdoor rustic
buildings is Romancing the
Woods of Woodstock, New
York, which offers gazebos,
pergolas, and other forms of
garden architecture. Their
structures are made of
durable locally cut cedar.

Opposite:
One of America's largest and
finest rustic structures,
the Old Faithful Inn at
Yellowstone National Park,
has thrilled visitors for
nearly a century.

A Source List for Rustic Furnishings and Decorative Accessories

Barney, Susan, and Erin Bellinger
Sampson Bog Studios
171 Paradise Point
Mayfield, NY 12117
518 661 6563

Barney and Susan are the quintessential rustic furniture makers. Barney works in the traditional Adirondack style, but provides the most innovative designs in the business. He adorns some of his furniture with paintings of outdoor scenes. He is widely regarded as the most accomplished builder/designer in the East.

Glen Burleigh
Box 106
Powell Butte, OR 97753
541 548 6913

Glen works with twisted juniper and makes furniture that falls into the realm of fantasy. His tables, chairs, railings, and other architectural elements are well made and innovative.

Chris Chapman Designs
0075 Deer Trail
Carbondale, CO 81623
970 963 9580

Chris Chapman is one of the great leather workers in the country. The frames for her mirrors are covered with hand tooled leather. The designs on the leather are original, well proportioned, and gorgeous.

Phil Clausen
Rt. 1 Box 3397
Coquille, OR 97423
503 396 4806

Phil Clausen has been passionately inspired by nature, in particular, mushrooms. His fantasy furniture offers high drama to any setting. He makes extraordinarily original pieces of maple, redwood, and other woods. His furniture, like that of all the other makers on this list, is highly sought after.

Diane Cole
10 Cloninger Lane
Bozeman, MT 59715
406 586 3746

Diane works in the traditional Western style and offers quality pieces from her workshop.

Jimmy and Linda Covert
907 Canyon Avenue
Cody, WY 82414
307 527 6761

Jimmy Covert is one of the master craftsmen in the West. His pieces are in museums and some of the finest private homes in the country.

Crystal Farms
18 Antelope Road
Redstone, CO 81623
970 963 2350

Crystal Farms constructs fine pieces of antler art.

Jerry and Jessica Farrell
Box 255
Sidney Center, NY 13839
607 369 4916

Jerry is known as the best mosaic artist in the business. His clocks are extraordinary. Jessica adds wonderful paintings that adorn much of Jerry's work.

Thom and Cloudbird George
PO Box 1827
Tonasket, WA 98855
509 486 1573

Thom and Cloudbird build furnishings from the shoots of willow and other saplings. Their works are sold privately and through galleries in the Rocky Mountains.

Barry Gregson
Charlie Hill Road
RR Box 88
Schroon Lake, NY 12870
518 532 9384

Barry Gregson is known as the best chair maker in the business. His chairs are comfortable, gorgeous, and guaranteed to last a lifetime. His other furnishings are of the same originality and perfection. Barry's sons and daughter are also involved in the business and make quality furniture in the Gregson tradition.

James Hanley
Box 219
Eganville, Ontario
K0J 1T0
613 628 3284

Jim offers traditional Adirondack style birch bark cupboards, bureaus, tables, mirrors, and other accessories. His pieces are uniquely designed and meticulously detailed.

Ken Heitz
Box 161, Rt. 28
Indian Lake, NY 12412
518 251 3327

One of the old-timers in the business, Ken works in the Adirondack style and has been turning out well made and well designed pieces for the past two decades.

R. C. Hink
PO Box 1142
Bellevue, ID 83313
203 788 6020

Rob specializes in cabinetmaking in the Western style. He is known for his meticulous and humorous interpretations of Western design.

Randy Holden
73 East Dyer Street
Skowhegan, ME 04976
207 474 7507

Randy Holden is a newcomer to the business, but his furniture offers some of the most original artwork in the field. Working with birch and other woods, he creates extremely imaginative pieces.

Beth Humphries
13084 Groman
New Buffalo, MI 49117

Beth creates traditional birch bark furniture in the Adirondack tradition.

Michael Hutton
RR2 Box 162
Pittsfield, IL 62363
217 285 5277

Mike offers some of the most original chairs and table in the country. The designs on his chairs are unique.

Jack Leadley
PO Box 142
Speculator, NY 12164
518 548 7093

Jack Leadley works in the Adirondack tradition building the best yellow birch rockers in the country. He uses no power tools and has no electricity in his shop. To own one of his chairs is a blessing.

Matt Madsen
PO Box 187
Orick, CA 95555
707 488 3795

Matt Madsen and Tim Duncan work on the West Coast with a variety of Western woods. They are best known for their wonderful freeform clocks, redwood slab chairs, and other furnishings.

Lionel Maurier
26 Tucker Mountain Road
Meredith, NH 03253-9627
603 279 4320

Lionel Maurier is a traditional rustic builder whose background in building log homes serves him well in making birchbark cupboards, apple settees, beds, and bureaus.

Brent McGregor
Kara Mickelson
Box 1477
Sisters, OR 97759
541 549 1322

Brent and Kara build some of the most extraordinary furniture in the West. Using mostly twisted juniper, they make beautiful beds, lamps, tables, and chairs.

Clifton Monteith
PO Box 165
Lake Ann, MI 49650
616 275 6560

Clifton Monteith is regarded as one of finest builders in the business. His furnishings, made from willow shoots, are exceptionally original, well made, and comfortable.

Nick Nickerson
PO Box 618
Copake, NY 12516
518 329 1664

Nick builds the most original picture frames working with a variety of tree barks. His frames seem to flow, enhancing any setting.

J. Mike Patrick
New West
2811 Big Horn Avenue
Cody, WY 82414
307 587 2839

Mike Patrick and his company, New West, produce very high quality Western furniture in the style of Thomas Molesworth.

Tom Phillips
Star Rt. 2
Tupper Lake, NY 12986
518 359 9648

Tom is one of the few people in the country who can build a great chair. He also makes exceptional tables and other items.

David Robinson
515 Tuxford Court
Trenton, NJ 08638
609 737 8996

David Robinson is the quintessential rustic gazebo and outdoor furniture maker. He works with cedar and makes some most extraordinary pieces.

Romancing the Woods
33 Raycliffe Drive
Woodstock, NY 12498
914 246 6976

Marvin Davis and Bob O'Leary offer the most romantic rustic garden architecture in the business. Their gazebos, pergolas, trellises, and outdoor benches are a positive addition to any garden, porch, or outdoor setting.

Lester Santos
2208 Public Street
Cody, WY 82414
307 587 6543

Lester creates original designs in the classic Western style. His furniture is exceptionally well made and very attractive. Many of the finest collections in the West have pieces made by Lester.

Ron and Jean Shanor
80 Hitching Post Drive
PO Box 1631
Cody, WY 82414
307 587 9558

Ron and Jean make innovative burled furniture in the Western tradition. Their products are sold through better galleries throughout the Rocky Mountains.

Doug Tedrow
Janice Smith
PO Box 3446
Ketchum, ID 83340
208 726 1442

Doug Tedrow and Janice Smith offer a significant innovation in rustic work—small pieces of wood are placed to resemble an interwoven pattern on their high quality furniture. Many of the top collections around the country are acquiring their furniture.

United Crafts
Sarah Wildasin
127 W. Putnam, Suite 123
Greenwich, CT 06830
203 869 4898

Sarah offers fine rustic and Arts and Crafts chinaware. The green matte finishes and raised pine cone motif on her wares blend extraordinary well into rustic settings.

Tom Welsh
PO Box 68
Minerva, NY 12851
518 251 4038

Tom has been a woodworker for several years and has recently added antler artwork to his offerings. His burled cherry chairs and tables are well constructed.

Peter Winter
PO Box 1082
Northville, NY 12134
518 863 6555

Peter Winter, a relatively new furniture maker, constructs most of his furniture of yellow birch in the Adirondack style. He offers some of the finest innovative designs on the East Coast. Many experienced collectors are adding Peter's furniture to their holdings.

Judd Weisberg
Rt. 42, Box 177
Lexington, NY 12452
518 989 6583

Judd is known for his well built furniture made from a variety of East Coast hardwoods.

A FEW SHOPS AND GALLERIES

Adirondack Store and Gallery
109 Saranac Avenue
Lake Placid, NY 12946
518 523 2646

A designer/decorator store that specializes in traditional rustic furnishings for the home.

Adirondack Trading Company
91 Main Street
Lake Placid, NY
518 523 4545

Their specialty is contemporary Rustic furnishings and accessories.

Black Bass Antiques
PO Box 788
Main Street
Bolton Landing, NY 12814
518 644 2389

Henry Caldwell specializes in antique fishing items and rustic decorative accessories.

Brookstone Antiques
9670 S. State Road 43
Brookstone, IN 47923
765 563 3505

This shop offers an extensive variety of rustic accessories as well as Indiana hickory furnishings.

Jerry Cohen
109 Main Street
Putnam, CT 06260
860 928 6662

Jerry Cohen has one of the largest Mission Oak shops in the country. He also handles marketing for Michael Adams of Aurora Studios who builds, by hand, fine reproduction Arts and Crafts lighting.

Fighting Bear Antiques
PO Box 3812
35 E. Simpson
Jackson Hole, WY 83001
307 733 2669

Terry and Sandy Winchell are the leading source for antique Thomas Molesworth furniture. They also carry a wide variety of rustic accessories, original American Indian objects and other antique furnishings. The Winchells have been responsible for furnishing some of the grandest ranches and residences in the West.

Michael Fitzsimmons Decorative Arts
311 W. Superior Street
Chicago, IL 60610
312 787 0496

Michael's gallery offers some of the best Arts and Crafts and Mission furnishings and decorative arts in the Midwest.

Martin Harris Gallery
60 E. Broadway
Jackson Hole, WY 83001
800 366 7814

Overlooking the main square in Jackson Hole, the gallery offers some of the finest rustic furnishings in the country.

Jordan Gallery
1349 Sheridan
Cody, Wyoming 82414
307 587 6689

The gallery specializes in high quality American Indian artifactss including blankets, rugs, beadwork, and numerous other items related to the West.

Ralph Kylloe Gallery
PO Box 669
Lake George, NY 12845
518 696 4100

This 7,500 square-foot log cabin gallery specializes in antique and contemporary furnishings and accessories for the home, resort, or business. The gallery features the works of many of the great rustic artists from all regions as well as offering antler chandeliers, old canoes, snowshoes, and a huge selection of decorative items.

Lodge Camp
PO Box 201593
Boulder, CO 80308
303 442 4094

Shawn Collins carries a large selection of antique rustic accessories as well as old canoes and related objects.

Mica Lamp Company
517 State Street
Glendale, CA 91203
818 241 7227

A skilled maker of mica lamp shades and accessories.

Moose America
75 Congress
Portsmouth, NH 03801
603 431 4677
and
Moose America
97 Main Street
Rangeley, ME 04970
207 864 3699

Specialists in rustic furniture and accessories.

Ross Bros.
28 North Maple Street
Florence, MA 01060
413 586 3875

Hank and Robert Ross deal largely in antique boats, including canoes, runabouts, and a wide variety of antique boating accessories. Their warehouse is extraordinary.

A Few Decorators Who Work in the Rustic Style

Associates III
1516 Blake Street
Denver, CO 80802
303 534 4444

Kari Foster has decorated more major
homes in the Rocky Mountains than anyone
else I can think of. Kari and her staff are
well respected in the field and have done
many outstanding homes.

Barbara Collum Decoration and Design
6976 Colonial Drive
Fayetteville, NY 13066
315 446 4739
315 369 2592

Barbara has worked on some of the most
extraordinary homes in the country. Her
Adirondack Great Camp is the envy of all
who visit.

A Few Fine Architects

Adirondack Design Associates
Michael Bird
77 Riverside Drive
Saranac Lake, NY 12983
518 891 5224

Michael was raised in the Adirondacks and
has designed some wonderful new homes in
the area. His style is classic Adirondack but
it integrates all the modern amenities.

Dwight Hudgins
True Log Construction
PO Box 219
Plainsboro, NJ 08536
609 799 9360

Dwight, an architect and log home builder,
creates original houses in the rustic style,
and provides absolute attention to detail—
as required by his many clients.

David Sellers
Box 288
Warren, VT 25674
802 496 2787

David does some of the most innovative
designs in the business. He often uses full
size trees (minus the branches) in his homes
to make an extraordinary statement.

Chair Weavers

Vito Decosmo
23 WestView Drive
Belchertown, MA 01007
413 323 7224

Vito is one of the old-timers in the business.
If he can't fix it no one can. He provides
high quality chair caning and weaving.

Kathi Pruitt
R#2 Box 297B
Morgantown, IN 46160
812 597 2440

Kathy has been reweaving hickory chairs for
many years. She knows what she's doing and
provides professional service.

Two Great Rustic Resorts

Manka's Inverness Lodge
PO Box 1110
Inverness, CA 94937
415 669 1034

Lake Placid Lodge
PO Box 550
Lake Placid, NY 12946
518 578 2700

Index

Page numbers in *italics* refer to captions and illustrations